A Simple Guide to Saving Your Family Photos

By Mollie Bartelt

Co-Founder of Pixologie

Pixologie . . . the study of life through your photos

Table of Contents

INTRODUCTION

Ever wonder why we put off organizing our photos to another day? Maybe we think a rainy day will come. Perhaps we plan to devote a week's vacation to sorting through and putting our photos in order.

It seems like organizing our photos should be easy, fun and full of laughter as we go down memory lane. But we know the reality is a lot different, as I have found over the years while helping people organize their photos. My friend Ann Matuszak and I founded a company called Pixologie - the first photo organization company of its kind in the country. Our mission focuses on helping people get their photos out of chaos and back into life to celebrate and share.

We've met many men and women who have been saving their photos for a very long time. In fact, saving photos is something most people are quite good at doing. Our clients save their printed pictures in a lot of different places. Any of these sound familiar?

- Shoeboxes, plastic containers, Ziploc bags, envelopes, photo boxes
- Under the bed, tucked in the nightstand or dresser, stacked in closets
- Photo albums (slide-in, magnetic, scrapbook, etc.)

But, are we really saving our photos?

I think something prevents many of us from moving forward on getting a handle on our pictures. . . Let's see if you can figure out what the reason is in these following stories from our clients:

✓ *Christine says, "I'd rather do manual labor all day than start organizing my old photos." She wanted to make a photo slideshow for her daughter's upcoming 40th birthday party. A grandmother who travels a lot, Christine described how her daughter's photos were mixed in many albums, boxes and folders. She had no idea how to start or how she'd make the time.*

✓ *Terry brought photos into our studio for a free scanning event we offered. She said, "I literally had the sweats last night figuring out which pictures to bring for scanning." She laughed, saying she almost needed a Xanax because it was so stressful for her.*

✓ *Mary hired us to help organize her photos. During our appointments, she often added new stacks and envelopes of photos to our piles. After two months of sorting and discarding, we scanned 3,768 photos for her. She told me during one of our visits, "There is no way I would ever have finished this without your help."*

Did you see a common theme in all of this?

People don't know how or where to start with getting their photos in order.

I wish this wasn't the case. Most of our clients find the reward of completing a photo organization project outweighs the work it takes. But many people never get started, or they start and stop every few years.

That is why I am writing this book . . . to offer the system we use at Pixologie. The system provides a simple way for anyone who wants to get printed photos under control. Then, the memories and stories can be enjoyed, shared and preserved for future generations.

A Little Background

Decades of accumulated photos, slides and negatives challenge consumers. In addition, the ongoing collection of digital photos being taken adds to the photo chaos. From a Suite 48 Analytics study entitled "The Photo Management Challenge," here is some industry statistics for you to know you are not alone in being overwhelmed by your photos!

- 57% of respondents believe their photo collections either need a lot of work or are largely disorganized.
- If they don't routinely sort through their photos to identify the worthwhile ones, 53% are bothered that they don't do this.
- Around 40% report not having the discipline to routinely sort through photos.

We see these stats in action every day at Pixologie to an even greater extent. Nine out of ten of the people we meet need some type of help with their photos, whether printed or digital.

How to Use This Book

I wrote this book in several chapters to set the stage for the multiple phases your photo organization project can go through.

First I'll share why saving your photos is so important and provide you with additional motivation to complete your photo organization project. Next, I'll outline the tools needed and touch upon what photos should be saved and what should be tossed. ***Please be prepared, you will need to throw some of your photos away!***

Then, I'll walk you through step by step how to organize your photos using the simple system we recommend and teach to our clients.

In the last two chapters, I will discuss how to save your photos and pass your photos on to future generations.

I invite you to skim, reread and double check the steps outlined in the book. While the steps are simple, photo organization is not a quick, easy task for most of us.

CHAPTER ONE - WHY SAVE YOUR PHOTOS?

Photos are so much more than a captured moment in time. They . . .

- Inspire
- Connect generations
- Strengthen families and children
- Celebrate life!

At Pixologie, Ann and I believe wholeheartedly in the power of family photos and preserving the stories captured in those pictures. Let me tell you more about what photos can do.

Photos Inspire

In 2015, Pixologie conducted an informal consumer study to learn how photos impact individuals and families. We found that 70% of our respondents stated photos help them get through tough times.

Their inspiring photos included memories such as:

- Completing 50-mile hikes and marathons
- Surviving cancer
- Serving as a missionary in a third world country
- And many more

One of our dear friends and clients, Bob Riley, inspires many people with his charitable works. Over the years he has raised hundreds of thousands of dollars for causes such as suicide prevention, homelessness, food kitchens, multiple sclerosis, a Honduran orphanage and much more.

Here is a photo of Bob at the top of Mount Kilimanjaro a few years ago. This amazing accomplishment involved months

of dedicated training. Bob's climb benefitted three charities and raised $60,000 for people in need. This photo captures his spirit, enthusiasm for life and dedication to helping people in need. It also shows how perseverance and hard work produces great results!

On a lighter note, I once spoke at a community event about organizing photos. During the class, I asked the attendees how their photos inspired them over the years. One woman mentioned, "Well, they inspire me to lose weight!" What a truth that is!

Photos Strengthen

Okay, you have piles of your children's (and maybe grandchildren's) photos in boxes, envelopes, tucked in bins in the closet. Maybe the photos are on your computer, different camera cards, smartphones and on Facebook! We know . . . you'll get to sorting the photos out someday. Well, we have some more reasons why you might not want to wait.

Your photos can be an excellent parenting tool in raising happy, well-adjusted children. Parenting and youth development expert, Deborah Gilboa, MD, (also known as Doctor G.) says that "organizing and displaying photographs connects children to our families, our values and our life goals for them."

I was fortunate to take part in a webinar with Doctor G who explained how this could be. Doctor G. believes that photos impact the three R's of parenting. In her experience, photos:

- Teach Respect
- Show Responsibility
- Build Resiliency

While the events and experiences of childhood help children grow and develop strong values, reflecting back on those moments is important. Parents can reinforce what their children have learned from those moments by looking back at the pictures and talking about the memories together.

Teaching Respect– In the photo below, we see my daughter feeding a deer. Looking back at the picture, we can help remind our children to treat all life with dignity and respect.

Showing Responsibility – A lover of animals, my daughter wanted to take this kitten home from a local petting zoo. It was free, and it was her birthday. But, I had to say no because I didn't think she was ready for the responsibility. We spoke about the kind of care the cat would need, and she reluctantly put him back. This moment leads into how photos help children become more resilient.

Building Resiliency – As we led Hannah out of the petting zoo, she was very sad even though the day had many fun moments. When children can work through their

disappointments, they become more resilient to the challenges life throws at them.

I bet you have many memories throughout your photo collection that can be teachable moments. When's the last time you looked at those pictures with you children? It's time to get your photos sorted to help grow strong, resilient children.

When we look at divorce statistics across the United States, a staggering number of weddings do not end happily. I understand many marriages require a parting of ways for emotional reasons, among other serious situations.

But, maybe, couples can avoid drifting apart over time by reminiscing over the good times shared together. We believe spending time smiling over photos can help strengthen a marriage, and strengthen a family.

Photos Celebrate Traditions & More

The majority of photos we organize deal with life's celebrations. This includes births, graduations, holidays, weddings and so much more. Photos hold the key to our traditions and provide an integral link to the past. The celebration of our traditions is extremely important today.

Life today in the 2010s is dramatically different from when I grew up with in the 1970s and 80s. There is no comparison to the lifestyles our grandparents lived in the 1930s, 40s and 50s. Our photos from the past show what life was like before the digital and technological revolution.

We need to preserve these photos so our children and their children learn about the important things in life . . . family and spending time together in an age where technology brought us together instead of apart.

In this photo, you can see my grandmother enjoying a canoe ride up north. This photo is special for a few reasons.

- Our family loved being up north when I was young (and we do now too!)
- My grandmother wore a dress for all occasions
- My sister (in the life jacket) did not remember this moment until she saw the photo a few years ago and it triggered a very special memory for her with our grandmother
- Life just seemed simpler back then

Think about the traditions you celebrate and consider where those photos might be. Here are a few traditions and celebrations we hope are in your collection of photos:

- Faith celebrations such as first Communions and Confirmations
- Holiday routines including Memorial Day observations or Fourth of July Parades
- School and sporting activities

Photos Connect Generations

In addition to celebrating traditions, photos connect the generations. You can see the world runs differently today than it did years ago. Our children need to hear about where they have come from, what values mattered to their family and how hard work builds character.

When completing a family history, we have found that photos are integral to telling a family's story. Photos add impact to family lineages by visually connecting generations. Children, teenagers and adults enjoy looking back at historical family photos when we take the time to do so.

Storm, Fire & Theft

Okay, maybe the emotional
rewards of preserving your photos
aren't motivating enough. You still
aren't feeling the drive to get those
photos out of chaos and safely
preserved. Let's talk about all the
things that can happen to your
photos.

Wildfires plague homeowners
out west, but a fire can occur
anywhere. What is the first thing grabbed when exiting a
burning home? Other than children and pets, the photo albums
are the priority. Even if the fire is contained and the house
saved, water damage to all the contents in the house can ruin a
photo collection.

Live in the Midwest or on the coasts? Flooding, tornados
and storms will damage or even steal your photos away forever.
As photo organizers, we hear heart-wrenching stories where
families have lost important photos and albums. Author and
professional organizer Jamie Novak writes in her book:

> *"I can't count the number of people who have reached out to
> me to share a story of how their photos met with a tragic fate:*

flooded basement, housefire, mold or they just became brittle and cracked. Each person felt guilty and regretted not having sorted and preserved their photos sooner." (Keep This, Toss That)

Did you know there is an organization that helps save photos lost in major storms? The National Photo Disaster Rescue organization has saved over 35,000 photos lost in key areas. When tornados hit in Missouri, Texas and Oklahoma, volunteers worked to gather photos from the wreckage, clean them and return the pictures to their owners. Learn more about NDPR at www.nationaldisasterphotorescue.com.

Don't let a disaster take your photos away from you. If you are reading this book, then you must have some desire to solve your photo mess. Make a plan to start saving your pictures today!

CHAPTER TWO – WHAT YOU NEED TO ORGANIZE YOUR PHOTOS

I'm going to be honest here . . . I did not title this book the "Quick" guide to organizing photos, because rarely is that the case. Organizing photos is a long-term commitment for the majority of people. Even with our help, some of my clients' photo organization projects have taken anywhere from three weeks to six months and more.

This chapter provides you with what you need to get your photos organized: Time, Space and Tools.

Time Commitment

What is your time frame? Can you commit to working on your photos at least an hour or two every few days? Or for a four-hour block on the weekend? Your success in completing your photo organization project depends on your ability to see the steps through.

You may want to set a timer for yourself. This will provide you with a set time you work on your photos and may let you know when your time is up. Time flies for me when I am sorting photos, so I need a reminder to stop!

Very important to remember, this is NOT the time to get caught up in memories. Take a step back from the personal memories, emotions and feelings. Once you start reminiscing about a photo, your time commitment just exponentially grows. During the sorting process, people who approach their photos neutrally or even critically have more success and less frustration.

> During the sorting of photos, approaching your photos unemotionally or even critically will save time in the long-run.

Have you tried organizing your photos before? Do you have half started piles from other times you attempted to sort your photos? Let this be the time you finish the organization. We'll give you the system, but in the end, your commitment is the ultimate indicator of success!

Space Required

Sorting through photos can consume a lot of space and time. If possible, you should ensure your space is an area where you can concentrate. The fewer chances for interruptions, the better.

Factors in determining where you will organize your photos include:

- how often can you work on your photos
- how much you need the space for life's other activities (like eating!)
- the ability of your family to leave your designated area alone

Ideally, you will want to have a dedicated table for your photos. A place where your photos can stay out for the duration of your organization is great. Some people are fortunate that they can dedicate a whole room to organizing photos. For working on your photos, you will need:

- A large flat space such as a kitchen table, but a six to eight-foot banquet table would be better

- Extra space such as chairs, shelves or counters to place bins of photos
- Storage shelves in a closet if you don't have room to keep your photos out when not working with them

Due to space limitations and personal preference, some of my clients only bring out their photo bins and boxes while I am there. In these instances, we work on specific sections of photos at a time.

Tools

Having the right tools on hand makes the photo organization process much easier. Here's our list of what you need with a description following.

- A variety of containers
- Long-term photo safe boxes
- Index cards
- Post-It notes
- Photo labeling pencil
- Spatula
- Dental floss
- Gloves
- Blue tape
- Age chart

Containers: Focus first on having the right number of containers for sorting your photos. You will need a variety of containers for short term sorting, fine-tuning organization and long-term storage. Examples include old photo boxes, shoe boxes, medium and large bins, wide, open Tupperware containers, etc.

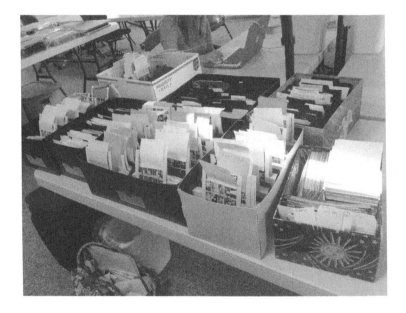

Short term boxes and bins during sorting process – also look at the Post-It notes being used!

Here's another example of a client with a variety of containers.

Long-term Storage: Okay, you have a good selection of containers for the sorting process. Some of those containers may be photo safe for the long-term storage of your photos once the organization is complete. If not, you will want to purchase photo safe, archival quality boxes.

We offer Legacy Boxes which hold up to 2,300 photos These are a true treasure to hand down to the next generation. In some cases, our clients use these boxes for their entire photo sorting process. The individual compartments and index cards are very user-friendly.

(See the ten divider compartments, 60 index cards, along with oversized envelopes to hold larger photos and protraits.)

Index cards – When stood on end in a container, index cards help section out photos and are extremely useful for sorting photos. You can write on the top of the index card labeling the section of photos the card precedes.

Post-It notes – We use sticky notes for several tasks such as labeling boxes and bins with large categories, writing notes for on the back of photos and much more. We recommend having a variety of the 3 x 3 inch size and the 1 x 2 inch size on hand.

Photo labeling pencil – These gentle, soft pencils provide a photo safe way to mark the back of photos with dates and names of the people in the picture. A more permanent solution than the Post-It note.

Spatula and dental floss – When you are removing photos from old sticky albums, a spatula comes in handy. Carefully slide under the photo. Then, while supporting the photo, pull the page away. Peeling stuck photos out of this type of album results in curled photos that are difficult to scan. For more precision, use dental floss to do the same task.

Gloves – You can
purchase white gloves from a
variety of places, including
Pixologie or even at Michael's
if their frame shop is willing.
When you handle old photos

that are crumbling, fragile and delicate, gloves are a must. The
oils from your hands and fingers will damage the photo further,
risking a tear, stain and more. Using gloves may prevent the
need for an expensive photo restoration of an important
heritage photo.

Blue tape – Oh, how we love our painter's tape! We use
this generously at our studio to help photo sorting clients divide
a table into sections. Then we label the tape with categories to
help our client organize photos further. The tape doesn't stick
permanently and provides a clear visual for clients who need
direction on how to start sorting photos.

Age chart – This tool provides ESSENTIAL clues to dating
pictures, especially for those people who have children (which
is most of the picture sorting population!). One of my clients has
four children – all of whom had a birthday party every year. I

couldn't imagine helping her with her photos without the age chart. Here's an example of an age chart:

Year	Child #1 - Mollie	Child #2 - Rosie
1972	Born 9/3/1972	
1973	1	
1974	2	Born 7/1/1974
1975	3	1
1976	4	2
1977	5 - Preschool	3
1978	6 – Kindergarten	4
1979	7 – 1st Grade	5 - Preschool
1980	8 – 2nd Grade, 1st Communion	6 – Kindergarten
1981	9 – 3rd Grade	7 - 1st Grade
1982	10 – 4th Grade	8 – 2nd Grade, 1st Communion
1983	11 – 5th Grade	9 – 3rd Grade
1984	12 – 6th Grade	10 – 4th Grade
1985	13 – 7th Grade	11 – 5th Grade
1986	14 – Graduated 8th Grade	12 – 6th Grade
1987	15 – Freshman	13 – 7th Grade
1988	16 - Sophomore	14 – Graduated 8th Grade
1989	17 - Junior	15 – Freshman
1990	18 – Graduated HS	16 – Sophomore
1991	19	17 – Junior
1992	20	18 – Graduated HS
Other Milestones	1994 – Graduated College 1996 - Wedding	1998 - Wedding

Keep in mind that the school years span two years. For this age chart, I used the year the child started that particular grade. For example, at age 15, Mollie entered her Freshman year in high school in 1987. Photos of her in her Freshman year, however, may span from September 1987 to June of 1988.

In this photo of young me, there are ten candles on the birthday cake. Looking at the age chart, I can see that I turned ten in 1982.

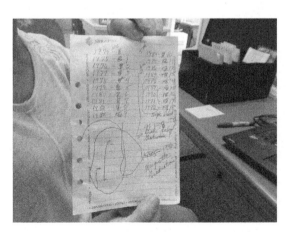

A handwritten age chart

If you are organizing a large collection of photos with multiple families, a more expansive timeline may be required.

Just apply the same principles of known dates and events (weddings, funerals, immigration dates, etc.)

Okay, we've covered the topics of time, space and tools. Now, we can dive into what photos you should save and then how to organize your photos!

CHAPTER THREE – WHICH PHOTOS SHOULD YOU KEEP?

Want to be successful in your photo organizing efforts? You will need to be OKAY with throwing away photos. For some people, this is extremely difficult, and others find it therapeutic. This chapter gives you strong permission to keep the photos you absolutely love and to get rid of photos that you don't need.

Some people ask for a specific number of photos they should save. Unfortunately, no magic formula exists on how many photos to save. It is also hard to picture (sorry for the pun!) what different quantities of photos look like. Based on experiences with my clients, here are some guidelines.

- One standard shoebox of photos holds approximately 1,000 photos.
- A frugal, efficient photo sorter will have one shoebox for each decade – roughly 100 photos per year. This

number of photos will capture a good section of the important times in your life.

- A passionate emotionally attached photo sorter will save approximately one shoebox for every two years. This means one decade will have 5,000 photos. In today's society where we can take more than 5,000 photos in one year, that doesn't seem like a lot!

- And there is everything in between – and there is no right or wrong answer here!

In the book "Downsizing the Family Home," author Marni Jameson writes,

"The goal of photos is to preserve memories, but no one wants to look through all the unedited photos of a lifetime."

Think of your role here as curator. You will pull the best photos and stories out of a generation or more of photos that future generations will be able to enjoy. How many photos can you look at and enjoy in one afternoon when the family gathers together?

For each client we have seen at Pixologie, the number of photos saved differs. A couple of examples include:

- Mary's Photo Organizing Project – 3,486 photos spanning the years of 1910 to 2010
- Bob's Photo Organizing Project – 9,500 photos spanning from the late 1800s to early 2000s
- Ken's Photo Organizing Project – 26,452 photos spanning the 1930s to early 2000s

General Recommendations

My "what to save" recommendations refer to photo collections in general. I have found that sometimes bad photos are the most precious to keep. So, with that being said, please use your heart and your judgment in determining what you want to save.

Keep every photo you absolutely love
even if it is of poor quality.

I offer the following points for you to think about which photos you can keep and which photos you can toss.

1. **Identifiable people** – your photo contains friends, family members and other acquaintances you know and want to remember.

   o Examples of photos you can toss – crowd settings where no one is recognizable and school activity photos where you cannot see your children

2. **Landscape, vacation, trips to the zoo, etc.** – Save if your photo contains family in it or a meaningful moment that you remember.

   o Examples of photos you may want to toss: landscape scenes you don't recall, vacation photos that are repetitive, most every zoo photo taken without a family member in the picture. I have to laugh at this because I took a photo of nearly every animal at Disney World's Animal Kingdom. I saved the two or three best animal photos and tossed the rest.

3. **Events like birthday parties and family reunions** – Save eight to ten of the best photos from events. Many

birthday parties occur year after year with a group of children and the photos tend to be repetitive and look the same. How many different angles of blowing out the candles on the cake do you need?

  o Examples of photos you may want to toss: unflattering angles of family members, all but one photo of the cake by itself, photos of people that are not relevant in your life anymore.

4. **Good quality photos –** Is your photo clear, in good condition?

  o Examples of photos you may want to toss: blurry photos, water damaged photos, sticky photos – with the understanding that if the photo is important to you, then save it.

Hopefully, this chapter has given you some clues on which photos you can toss. The more photos you can weed out of your collection, the easier the organization will go.

Now we move on to how to organize your printed photo collection!

CHAPTER FOUR – HOW TO ORGANIZE YOUR PHOTOS

We have used our photo organization system with clients since the beginning of our company. We have also taught our system to hundreds of people over the years and have received positive feedback.

I'll break down our system steps in much more detail, but I want you to see how the system works overall. Let's touch upon our simple system for organizing photos in a nutshell. Here it is:

1. Bring all of your photos to one place
2. Sort all photos by major category
3. Then breakdown each major category's photos into subcategories
4. Fine tune subcategories as desired

As you can see, you will be sorting through your photos in phases. It is possible you'll be handling your photos anywhere from two to four or more times, depending on your organizing style. Whenever possible, throw away photos that are obviously duplicates, bad pictures, repetitive in nature, etc. You will appreciate having less to sort in the final step of organization.

Once you have sorted and organized your photos into their final place, you will want to scan them into digital files. We cover scanning in Chapter Five.

Step One - Bring It All Together

In our Pixologie Printed Photo Organization classes, we teach our attendees to collect their photos in one place as the first step. Even if you are not starting right away, bringing all the photos together is a great beginning.

Just to remind you - all your photos include: albums, boxes of photos, baggies of photos, bins of photos, envelopes of photos, old framed photos in closets, school portraits and any other place you have photos stashed. Have drawers of photos? It's time to empty those out into one of the bins we mentioned in the tool section.

Why bring it all together?

1. Seeing your photos all together helps provide perspective on what needs to be completed.

2. Treating this project as an "all or nothing" venture provides you with a clear goal.

3. Identifying and tossing duplicates become much easier.

4. Enjoying the final organization is much more satisfying knowing the family's printed photos are sorted and safe.

Now, realistically, you will continue to find photos as you start your photo organization project and into the future. Add these to a "To Be Sorted" bin or section of your table for the time being as you collect them. In the beginning, everything will need to be sorted, but as you progress, the "To Be Sorted" will grow smaller.

THE PHOTO ALBUM DILEMMA

Okay, if you have photos in albums, I bet you are wondering, "What's the plan for these?"

If you want to "save" your photos for future generations, your photos have to come out of the albums at least temporarily for organization and scanning.

The decision of whether to put the photos back into albums lies with you. Here are some questions to consider:

- Do I want to have these albums forever?
- Will my kids want these albums?
- Are my photos safe in them?
- Are these albums in good condition?
- Will I want or need to downsize my home someday?
- As you look through photo albums, do any photos stand out that you no longer need to save?

Remember, back in the day; it was normal to save every photo taken because we had so few to look through. If you do decide to continue using photo albums, chances are, you'll want to get rid of poor quality photos and place the good pictures in new, photo safe albums.

For our clients at Pixologie, in some cases, we remove the photos from albums and throw away the deteriorating albums. In other cases, clients want to have their photos returned to their albums after organization and scanning. We don't often perform this service because it is so incredibly time intensive to put pictures back into albums. Also, returning pictures to unsafe photo albums defeats the entire purpose. For those clients, we

have seen their best intentions fail . . . meaning they now have to store the empty old albums along with the photos they have not put back into the albums. This situation creates a further mess in the future. It is your call, but we have seen that people who intend to put pictures back in their albums often never get to it.

We'll be rooting for you either way – but we have found the most popular option is to purchase an elegant heirloom quality photo safe box to store the photos.

Here, these photos have been pulled from dated albums and secured with a rubber band. If you are interested in returning your photos to their albums, this system worked well for temporary storage and transport. We have also seen people put their photos in dated legal sized envelopes for grouping and later to return to albums.

NEGATIVES AND SLIDES

As you are bringing your photos together, you may find negatives and slides. We include these in our photo organization projects. However, the two have very different outcomes generally.

Negatives – Do you have negatives still stored in envelopes? You can get rid of them if the photos are in the envelopes with the negatives or if you know for sure you have the photos already.

If the negatives are not with their photos and you are unsure if you have the photos, place the negatives in a bin and set to the side. Leave the negatives in their envelope and any documentation, if possible.

Negatives can be extremely expensive to have reprints made or to have scanned (from 89 cents to $5 each). We try to figure out what we might be missing in our photo collection before determining if we need to scan the negatives.

Slides – Well, there is good news and bad news about slides. Generally speaking, people in the 1960s, 70s and 80s did not have prints made of their slides. That's good news, so you don't have to worry about matching duplicate printed photos with their slides.

The bad news is that if you have slides, you probably have hundreds of slides, maybe even thousands. Extremely popular during their time, slides offered families the ability to have photos shows in their living rooms.

As with negatives, reprinting or scanning slides can be costly depending on what type of service you use. If you have slides, set them aside for the time being.

EXAMPLES OF PEOPLE BRINGING ALL THEIR PHOTOS TOGETHER

Here are some photos of people bringing it all together! How do these photo collections compare with your current photo situation?

*One client's collection: 55 photo albums and
many other containers of photos.*

*Sometimes people collect all of their photos
and store them in suitcases.*

*Here's Ken's photo organizing project - a great example of how to
sort one box at a time into major categories.*

Step Two - Organize by Major Category

If we went about organizing our photos into all the separate events and moments in our lives, we truly would never finish sorting our photos. Our next step after bringing all the photos together is to organize the pictures by major category.

Choosing Your Photo Categories – This is the most important part of the project. You'll want to carefully consider what categories you'll use when organizing your photos. Halfway in, changing your mind will seriously dampen your enthusiasm in getting through those piles of pictures.

We recommend organizing photos chronologically for several reasons:

1. Most importantly – cross-referencing photos by date is so much easier when you have similar or duplicate photos to compare.

2. You can refer to your Age Chart when not sure of a date and file your photo more accurately in a chronological system.

3. When your photos are digitized, they can be labeled with the date and searched for by date.

4. With facial recognition available in many photo programs (not Windows Photo Gallery as of yet), you

will have the technology to simplify identifying people in photos.

However, we have seen successful photo organization projects when organized by person or other methods. Here are other major category types you might consider for sorting your photos.

- Chronologically (Decades)
- Subject (Family, Vacation, Sports, Events, Work and others)
- Person (Mom, Dad, First Child, Second Child, etc.)
- Holiday (Valentine's Day, Easter, Fourth of July, Thanksgiving, Christmas and more)
- Album, box or source (Red Album, Alaska Album, Grandma's Box of Photos – essentially, naming the bin by where your photos were originally)
- Photo type, shape and age (heritage photos, the 1930s & 1940s photos, square rounded photos, etc.)

One of my clients, Mary, wanted to organize her photos by person despite my reservations. She was certain that she wanted to organize her photos by person. She explained she would be looking for her photos primarily by who was in the pictures. Her system worked very well. It was great to see how fast she could work by sorting her pictures by who was in the photo. In the end, we sorted her photos by person as the major category and organized them by date for the subcategories. She was thrilled with the result.

A couple of observations from organizing photos by person:

- PRO FOR ORGANIZING BY PERSON - Mary can easily find photos of each one of her children. In fact, one daughter is getting married this fall, and she easily will be able to create a photo slideshow for the reception. (I scanned the photos and saved them into digital folders organized by person as well.)
- CON FOR ORGANIZING BY PERSON - Photos from special family events will be split across four to five different categories depending upon who is in the photo. If you want all the photos from one of your family events, you would have to search through each person's photos to find those pictures.

It is up you to determine how you can best use your photo collection. The accomplishment will still feel as great when your photos are sorted, no matter the categories you used to sort them!

EXCEPTIONS TO YOUR CATEGORIES

School Portraits - No matter which set of categories you choose, when you encounter portrait photos (school, church, professional, etc) always set those aside into a bin labeled "Portraits."

If you are like many other people, your portrait photos will be scattered all over the place with many duplicates and different sizes. Portraits should be kept separate for easier

sorting at a later date once ALL of your photos have been located throughout your house and sorted into their major categories! It's just a quick tip that has helped us save time.

OPTIONAL – Separate your immediate family member school portraits from the portraits you received from your extended family and friends. Some of these from outside your family may be okay to throw away or return to the family who gave it to you.

Photos of Other People You Don't Want Anymore – Most of my clients set aside photos of others that they'd like to give to those people who are in the pictures. If you are going to do this, create a bin labeled something like "Give to Someone Else" and put all the photos that you want to give away in that bin.

AN EXAMPLE OF MAJOR CATEGORIES

Here's a list of the major categories created by one of my clients – you'll see photos on upcoming page:

- Heritage Photos (Mom's Side)
- Heritage Photos (Dad's Side)
- 1950s
- 1960s
- 1970s
- 1980s
- 1990s
- 2000s
- 2010s
- Portraits
- Photos To Give Away
- Husband's Work Photos

SYSTEM TO ORGANIZE PHOTOS BY MAJOR CATEGORY

1. Choose your categories and label your bins for placing the corresponding photos
   - Create bins for the categories as you go along
2. Pick a section, an album, box or envelope of photos to start organizing into the bins
   - OPTIONAL – use index cards to group photos – don't let it slow you down
3. Sort those photos into the corresponding bin categories **DISCARDING the bad photos, duplicates, etc. right away.** (Remember, don't reminisce!)
4. Complete that set of photos, decide if you are moving on to a new batch of photos to organize
5. Repeat the steps until all your photos have been sorted into a major category
6. Don't forget to keep tossing photos

Here's a set of bins. Back row – 1980s, 1990s, 2000s. Front row – Portraits, 1970s, Garbage. With a few slides found in the mix from one drawer of photos.

EXAMPLE: CHRONOLOGICAL PHOTO ORGANIZING

The boxes from left to right read "1960s, 1970s, 1980s and 1988."

1988 had so many photos already separated; we just added a box to hold those particular photos. You can also see some index cards and Post-It notes where I separated years that were obvious (because they came out of neatly organized albums which the client discarded after removing the photos.) The albums in front of the 1970s are from the 1970s but have individual notes with each photo and we haven't decided how to proceed with those. We set the albums with the other 70s pictures for now. Below the table is a photo box holding negatives and an office paper box filled with more envelopes of negatives. We will look through those once we get through organizing the majority of her photos.

In this photo, you can see my client's other bins of photos on her table and the back shelf of her dining room.

Each time I visit we tackle another box or two of photos to sort.

There are also two extremely large bins of the gallon size Ziploc bags of photos underneath her table with close to 5,000 photos labeled by year which is extremely helpful.

EXAMPLE: PHOTOS ORGANIZED BY PERSON

In the photos above, you can see Mary's boxes of photos sorted by person and already organized by her subcategories. During Step Two, there were no subcategory index tabs with dates on them. All of the photos were disorganized and had to be sorted extensively.

You are looking at Mary's final organization here. Mary finished her organization extremely fast due to her ability to quickly look at a photo, toss it if necessary and move on to the next picture.

WRAPPING UP STEP TWO – ORGANIZE BY MAJOR CATEGORY

I can't tell you how long Step Two will take because it depends entirely on you! Will you be a "Super Sorter" and zoom through your photos, tossing the duplicates, bad photos and repetitive photos quickly and decisively? I have seen clients finish their initial sorting into categories in a weekend. Others have taken a lot longer.

There is no award for the best organizing job or fastest job! The goal is to simply finish Step Two. Don't quit!

Step Three - Break Major Categories Down

Okay, we've reviewed sorting all of your photos into their major categories. Now we can fine tune each major category into subcategories of the organization. Again, as you go through these photos for the second time, continue to toss photos as you can. At this point, you should start remembering photos and getting a sense of what duplicates you come across.

Chronological Category Breakdown – If you sorted your photos by decades to start with, now is the time to break the decades into years where possible. From the same client I talked about before, here are where her decades are broken down into years now.

In this photo, you can see we have started dividing up the 1980s photos into years. Note that we have several index cards with an "undated" label. We may never figure those dates out more precisely than the decade.

Also note in the back an index card labeled "Photo Cards." These are similar to the category of "Portraits" and I'd recommend separating them from your photo collection as well. The original photo you used on the card SHOULD stay in your photo collection. Some clients like to have their holiday photo cards stored together in order.

The 1990s photos were broken down by year in this photo. Remember the Ziplock bags of photos under our client's table? Each Ziplock bag was labeled with the year the photos were taken. So, our next step was to incorporate those bags of photos into the photos we had organized from other places earlier in our process.

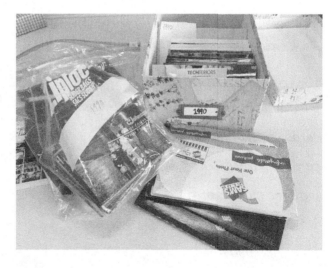

You can see that the 1990s had two bags of photos and the box labeled 1990 need to be consolidated, de-duplicated and the envelopes tossed.

TIP – if you are sorting, use index cards to transfer the information on the envelopes (if any). This way you can get rid of the photo envelopes which are a hindrance to easily viewing photos in your boxes and take up space.

Further Chronological Category Breakdown – Some people find that sorting by year provides a great level of organization, and they are content to stop the sorting at this point. I like to go one step further and organize by month within the years especially in the 1980s and 1990s because duplicates were so prevalent during those decades.

Once you have sorted your photos from decades into years, the next step is to sort by months. This part may seem tedious, but it is the final step in organizing your photos and can provide your photo organization project with a very high level of accurate organization by date and duplicate removal.

Here you can see I have laid out index cards. Each of these cards is labeled with the months of 1990 (1990 – January; 1990 – February, etc.)

I also have included an index card labeled 1990-Undated for photos of indeterminate month. Then I have started sorting the photos by month. Context clues (Easter, Halloween, etc.) and markings on the back made sorting fairly easy. When dealing with a year's worth of photos for the first time, it is easier to sort them onto the flat table before moving your stacks into the box.

I have stacked the organized photos in the photo box by the months in 1990. In the back, the last index card includes the undated photos. My client will review these on our next visit, and she will attempt to put them in the months they belong if possible.

Also note, I realized that I hadn't sorted the photos from the second Ziploc bag. Fortunately, it was easy to sort these photos into the others already organized since I used the same context clues and recognized some of the events from the other photos I had sorted.

EXAMPLE OF STEP THREE – SORTING BY SUBCATEGORY CHRONOLOGICALLY

Remember my client's back table of bins labeled by decade? We have made significant progress here.

Once you have sorted your photos chronologically down to the month where possible, it is easier to add the random photos in your "To Be Sorted" bin. It's great to grab a photo, go to the month and find other photos from the same event.

OTHER CATEGORY TYPES BROKEN DOWN INTO SUBCATEGORIES

You will find many different options of how to break down the other types of categories. As you go through your photos, no doubt other subcategories will come to light. Here are some ideas for you.

SORTING BY SUBJECT: Major Categories/Subcategories

- **Family** – Grandparents, parents, children, pets
- **Vacation** – Locations, types of vacations (cruise, in-state, European), Who you traveled with
- **Sports** – Children's activities, school sports
- **Events** – Holidays (breakdown to individual holidays) reunions, weddings, birthday parties, faith events
- **Work** – Co-workers, work events, awards and recognition

In the photo to the right, we are looking at the photo box with vacation pictures, sorted by the places where the couple had traveled.

SORTING BY PERSON: Major Categories/Subcategories

- Self – (you can simply organize these photos by date, or you can break them down by different categories as well.) Ideas include: growing up, dating years, marriage, raising children, life without children, travel, etc.)
- Spouse
- Parents
- Child (individual children, group photos of children; hobbies, etc.)
- Extended Family (sort by family groups)
- Family Friends
- Specific Family Activities that Are Traditions (camping, waterskiing, sporting events)

These categories and subcategories are interchangeable, meaning you don't have to be completely bound by one method or the other. For instance, I sort my photos chronologically as a rule. However, last year I collected a bunch of photos of my aunt from various places to create a photo poster board for her birthday. I don't store them chronologically since I don't know their date taken, and they are not part of any event my family attended. However, I have stored them in a folder labeled with her name, in case I need them in the future or another family member wants copies of them.

You can sort chronologically but have a separate container of photos for very special pictures. One of my clients pulled out baptism photos and differentiated them because her children were at the stage of having babies and being able to share the baptism photos easily was important.

SORTING PORTRAITS AND HOLIDAY PHOTO CARDS

Whichever major categories you choose to sort, you will probably have bins with portraits and holiday photo cards.

- Portraits (Subcategories include: Immediate Family, Extended Family and Friends) – then sort by person and then by year, tossing the duplicates which may be plentiful. I never felt right about throwing the extra portraits of my children away, but there comes a time when it is okay to let those dinky wallet size extras go!

- Holiday Photo Cards (Subcategories include: Family, Extended Family and Friends.) Then sort by year. You don't have to save the 25 extra cards you never sent, just save a couple and keep them all in one place in your photo collection.

Question – Here's a school portrait of my dad from 1952. Would I sort this into portraits or my heritage photos?

Answer – Good question. I tend to put all photos of my parents into a bin categorized as "Heritage Photos," even the portraits. And I would apply that rule of thumb to all those ancestor type photos I may come across.

SPECIFIC STEPS TO BREAKDOWN INTO SUBCATEGORIES

1. Take one bin with a major category and separate photos into the subcategories you have identified.
2. Label and use index cards to separate the subcategories
3. Eliminate doubles and bad photos where possible
4. Repeat until all major categories have been sorted into subcategories
5. If desired, further sort subcategories

Step Four – Final Review

Okay – you have finally sorted and combed through your photos at least two times, if not more. Do you feel like your photo collection is set for the scanning process? We like to have people go through their photos one last time to weed out any final photos that may be unnecessary to keep.

Remember our client with the 55 photo albums and numerous other containers? We estimate that we started with 13,000 photos to organize. After Steps Two and Three, we had narrowed the photo collection down to around 10,000 photos.

During our Final Review, with our client's input, we tossed an additional 500 photos – and eliminated one entire Legacy Box from the five pictured here down to four boxes.

EXAMPLE: MARY'S PHOTO STORAGE AFTER HER FINAL REVIEW

The bin with the "empty" label is filled with the family's photo calendars and is just waiting for a neatly printed label.

Remember: Your photo organization journey does not end when your photos are sorted and stored neatly. You need to backup your photos digitally to ensure your memories are preserved and protected. This leads into our next chapter: How To Save Your Photos.

Special Note: Slides and Negatives

Remember, we set aside the slides and negatives? Now that you are a photo organizing pro, you can sort through your slides. You can use a light box to sort and keep the best of the slides. The light box may also help with determining if you need to save any of your negatives.

Here are a few tools we use when working with slides and negatives.

An old fashioned light box for sorting slides and a Wolverine Slide & Negative scanner.

CHAPTER FIVE – HOW TO SAVE YOUR PHOTOS

Now that your photos are organized, it's time to save your photos. Let's define what "Save" means. For this book, I consider a photo saved when it meets both of these conditions:

1. It is stored in an organized fashion, and you can find the photo when you need or want it – We've shown you how to do this.

2. It is backed up in two other places – a location within your home and a location outside of your home such as a family member's home, a safe deposit box or the cloud.

If either of these conditions is not met, your photo is in danger of being lost to time, disaster or other unfortunate situation.

NUMBER ONE - STORED IN AN ORGANIZED FASHION

If Number One is not met, situations will arise when you are looking for certain photos, and you cannot find the pictures.

These situations center around major family events when sharing photos and memories matters the most. We've had clients with the following situations:

- Funeral of a parent – A family must rush around to find photos of their mother or father for the funeral home. Some of the photos are on copy paper from an ink-jet printer. No one knows where the originals are and the photos are poor in quality.

- Celebration of a wedding anniversary – A daughter must take a photo of a picture in a frame to include that special memory in a photo slideshow.

- High school graduation – We've had several clients with children graduating from high school or college who must scramble at the last minute to put together photo boards.

It's interesting to see how many of my clients have groupings of photos from different events over the years adding to their photo chaos. Invariably, when photos are pulled out for this type of project, the pictures are not returned to their proper place.

Does this sound familiar? For those of you who have already organized your photos, did you have envelopes of certain family members that had been used for a special event?

NUMBER TWO – BACKED UP IN TWO OTHER PLACES

If your photos are not backed up in two other places, your photos could be lost to fire, floods, theft and other types of damage. We've seen the following situations at Pixologie:

- A basement flood soaks wedding photos which were thought to be stored in a water tight container.
- A fire destroys a home and all of its contents. The family must rely on relatives to provide copies of pictures.
- A smartphone is stolen, with hundreds of special holiday photos gone forever
- A box of photos is lost during a move

So far, through this book, we have talked about organizing printed photos. It is not realistic to have two printed copies of your photo collection. When considering how to back up your photos in two places, we are now referring to creating a digital copy of your printed photos. Digital copies are created by scanning your entire printed photo collection. Once you have the digital copies, you can easily store the copies in two locations.

Scanning Your Photos

Over twenty years ago, the first scanners became available. I remember my dad's first flatbed scanner purchase which was well over $1,000. We were so excited about the ability to scan photos and other documents.

Flash forward to the present, we find most households have the potential to scan pictures with their printers. However, the majority of people I meet don't scan their photos because they don't know how or they find the process too slow.

Fortunately, technology has come a long way, and faster scanners are available now. When you scan a photo, you want to end up with a digital file that is a JPG (most everyone) or a TIFF (advanced users). Please see Appendix B for recommended scanning settings.

Here's a quick overview of the different scanning options available.

PORTABLE SCANNERS

From wand-type scanners to the Flip-Pal Mobile scanner, these options offer simplicity and convenience for scanning photos. You don't need a computer to scan photos with these devices. For the most part, scanners like these cost below $200.

With wand type scanners, you simply feed the photos through the slot. The digital images are captured on a camera SD card. You can then transfer the photos from your card to your computer. Typically, wand scanners do need a power supply.

The Flip-Pal Mobile scanner allows you to scan photos wherever you are. While it's flatbed only fits 4 x 6 photos, the Flip-Pal comes with software to stitch scanned sections of a larger photograph together.

The Flip-Pal has a small screen so you can see your photo as it is scanned.

PRINTER SCANNERS

Yes, you can scan photos with your printer/scanner in a pinch if you need. However, we recommend this method of scanning only when it is necessary. A few years back, I had to scan around 400 photos for a family member's funeral with a printer scanner. Scanning a large number of photos is inexpensive but the job took over six hours to complete and it was frustrating. Using your printer to scan a large number of photos takes a very long time. Other scanning options cost more but are way more efficient.

Typically, your printer scanner comes with software that allows you to save your scans in a folder on your computer.

FLATBED PHOTO SCANNERS

Early on in helping people with their photos, we relied on our flatbed photo scanner. Coming with their own photo scanning software, these scanners often allow you to scan multiple pictures at the same time but then save each picture separately as a JPG.

Also, you will find there are more options in how you save photos to your computer and how you name your files.

But, these scanners also are time-consuming to use.

HIGH-SPEED PHOTO SCANNERS

When you have more than a few hundred photos to scan, a high-speed photo scanner will make life very easy for you. We use the Kodak Alaris Picture Saver Scanning System (Kodak Alaris PS80) which scans up to 85 photos a minute! Yes, the Kodak Alaris PS80 scans at an unbelievable speed. The PS80 scans faster than we can keep up with it.

The Kodak Alaris Picture Saver Scanning Systems start around $1900 which is cost prohibitive for many people. At Pixologie, we rent the scanners anywhere from an hour up to a week to people who want to scan photos fast without the cost of a full purchase. Clients who rent typically can scan around 1,000 to 1,200 photos per hour.

Nationwide, people can rent the scanners through our favorite colleagues, E-Z Photo Scan with their Rent2Scan program. This company is the largest distributor of Kodak Alaris Picture Saver Scanning Systems and are the go-to experts in selling, renting and supporting the scanners.

You can find their contact information in the Resources at the end of this book.

Our local FOX television station featured us on air demonstrating the PS80. Many people have no idea this scanning equipment exists. We hope to  *spread the word far and wide that there is an easier way to scan photos.*

After reviewing the types of scanners that are available, does the thought of scanning photos overwhelm you? Or, do you not have the equipment to scan the photos easily? That's okay.

HIRE SOMEONE TO SCAN YOUR PHOTOS

There are many providers who will scan your photos for you. Most options involve shipping your photos somewhere to have the work done. This can be nerve wracking for some who worry the photos may be lost in the journey.

We love to help people scan their own photos if possible either at home, in our studio or with another Pixologie owner.

Another great resource if you don't have a Pixologie in your area is the the Association of Personal Photo Organizers. If you are looking for someone locally to help you organize and scan photos, go to www.appo.org. You will find resources and a directory of personal photo organizers around the country.

When you hire someone to help you with your photo projects, we recommend asking for two references. If you are using an online scanning service, please Google their name and read their reviews.

Lastly, I have included Appendix B – Best Practices for Your Photos where you can see our recommendations for saving your photos and other media.

Creating Two Back-Ups of Your Photos

Once you have scanned your photos, you'll have your original digital files stored on your computer. We recommend that two additional copies be made. One copy can be stored in your home, and the other should be stored outside of your home. Having copies in two locations ensures your photos are safe even if you have a disaster at home.

A variety of external hard drives

FIRST COPY – Simply copy your scanned photos to an external hard drive. Remember to update your back-up on the external hard drive if you scan additional photos on your computer.

SECOND COPY – Should be stored outside of your home. A couple of options include:

- A second external hard drive. Store it in a safe deposit box or at a family relative's home

- Cloud back-up. There are many computer back-up services available including Carbonite and Backblaze. These services back up all of your computer's files. In the event of a computer crash, the company will send your files back for you to restore to your computer. *Cautionary note: Please do not depend upon a cloud service being your **ONLY** photo back-up. While Carbonite and Backblaze have been around a long time, many technology companies have come and gone. Also, we have heard client stories where the back-up they counted on did not work properly and photos were lost.*

- Photo specific cloud services – I'll address the free services later in this book but I'd like to draw your attention to one unique company that we've been watching and telling our clients about – Forever.

Here's a little bit about Forever from their website: *With Forever, you can edit, organize, store, and share your photos. Rest easy knowing your content will always be safe in your permanent digital home at Forever. All of this is possible because of the Forever Guarantee and our easy-to-use web, mobile, and desktop apps.*

We have covered a lot of topics related to managing the chaos of our printed photos including:

✓ *Why we should save our printed photos*

✓ *What tools we need to organize our photos*

✓ *What photos should we keep*

✓ *How to organize our photos*

✓ *How to save our photos by creating digital back-ups*

The vast majority of our clients report they have a digital mess of photos as well as their printed pictures. Since we have created digital photos of our printed pictures, I want to talk about how to save digital photos. Let's head on to the next chapter.

CHAPTER SIX – HOW TO SAVE YOUR DIGITAL PHOTOS

Although I am writing this book primarily about printed photo organization, I did want to address digital photo management for a few moments. Remember how we brought all of our printed pictures to one location? We want to do the same thing for our digital photos. Here's a brief list of where you'll be grabbing all the photos you want to keep:

- Laptop computer
- Desktop computer
- Smartphone (camera, text messages)
- External hard drive
- Jump drives/thumb drives
- DVDs/CDs
- Email
- Social media (Facebook, Instagram)
- Camera/Camera SD Cards

Bringing All the Digital Together

While cloud-based solutions are numerous, some consumers are not ready to embrace iCloud, Google Photos, and many others yet. So, the most common place we see people storing their digital photos is on computers, smartphones and in social media accounts. We need to bring all the digital photos together in one place if we want to get rid of our digital mess!

Today, the most logical place to save your digital photo collection is on your personal computer. This means you will need to make a strong effort to transfer photos from your smartphone, social media accounts and camera to your computer on a routine basis.

We recommend, at a minimum, that you bring your photos to your computer at the end of each month. For both PC and Mac computers, you should store your photos in the "Pictures" folder.

You can do much more with your photos than simply getting them to one place where they can be backed up. PCs and Macs offer free photo software solutions which allow you to correct red eyes and crop your pictures.

- PC – Photo Gallery
- Mac – Photos

There are many online videos to watch so you can learn how to get the most out of these programs. You can also find community classes to take as well.

For people who want even more power to work with their photos, we've enjoyed using these programs with our clients as well:

- Forever Historian (PC)
- Mylio (PC and Mac)
- Forever Guaranteed Storage (PC and Mac)

Steps for Saving Your Digital Photos

At least monthly, follow these steps to save your digital photos.

1. Review your wonderful photos (all of them – see the list of places you might be accumulating digital photos at the beginning of this chapter.)

2. Delete the ones you don't want. RIGHT AWAY!

3. Transfer or download the photos to your computer and save in your Pictures file in a file folder labeled for the month you are saving your photos.

4. Use this suggested file format – YYYY-MM-DD (example: 2015-10-31 Halloween)

5. Review again and delete unneeded photos

6. Then share to your social media, order prints, etc. and enjoy.

7. Back up your photos twice (one copy saved in the house; one copy saved outside the house)

Think of all the times you may have taken a photo and skipped to the sixth step. Many, many photos have been lost since the digital revolution because people take their photos, maybe share their photos and never get them organized or properly backed up.

Naming Your Digital File Folders

I want to expand on how to name your digital file folders. We recommend the naming convention of YYYY-MM-DD - Description – which will help your folders display in date order properly. For example:

2014-12-10 Christmas Concert

2014-12 December Phone Photos

2014 – Social Media Downloaded Photos

See the listing of some of my file folders below. You can see how I named my file folders and how I split photos up into events.

Name	Date Modified
2015-05 Hannah's Band Concert	Mar 12, 2016, 7:28 PM
2015-05 Junior National Honor Society	Aug 8, 2015, 4:53 PM
2015-05 Other May Photos	Mar 12, 2016, 7:28 PM
2015-05 Tammy's House	Jun 1, 2015, 2:14 PM
2015-06 Alex Rides a Bike	Jan 31, 2016, 6:09 PM
2015-06 June Photos	Aug 3, 2015, 9:12 PM
2015-07 Hannah's Band Camp	Oct 24, 2015, 8:37 PM
2015-07 July Photos	Nov 27, 2015, 5:18 PM
2015-07 Trip to Alaska	Nov 27, 2015, 5:01 PM
2015-07-01 Alex Testing	Aug 3, 2015, 7:46 PM
2015-07-11 Family Reunion	Oct 24, 2015, 9:37 PM
2015-08 August Photos	May 28, 2016, 9:48 PM
2015-08 Last Day of Summer Vacation	Oct 24, 2015, 8:10 PM
2015-08 Magnolia Ridge	Nov 27, 2015, 5:59 PM
2015-08 Salon Day	Dec 28, 2015, 7:50 PM

Adding Scanned Photos to Your Digital Collection

You may be wondering how to add your scanned photos to your digital collection. Depending on your computer savvy and your desire, you can:

- Leave the scanned pictures separate from your other digital folders in your Pictures File
- Create dated folders and move your scanned photos into the years they belong
- Import the scanned photos into your photo management software

The possibilities are endless due to the huge number of photo editing software and apps available for consumers.

Backing Up Your Digital Photos

As with backing up your scanned photos, we recommend two back-ups of your computer's digital photo collection.

FIRST COPY – Copy your Pictures file to an external hard drive. Remember to update your back-up on the external hard drive every time you add photos to your Pictures file.

SECOND COPY – Should be stored outside of your home. A couple of options include a second external hard drive and/or Cloud backup as discussed in Chapter Five.

iCloud Considerations

With many, many consumers using iPhones and iPads to take pictures, I would like to point out a few things about iCloud.

- Every iPhone and iPad owner has an iCloud account. You can go to icloud.com and use your Apple ID to log into your account. By clicking on the Photos icon, you will see your photos stored in iCloud.

- I have seen people with multiple iCloud accounts because they have signed up different devices with different email accounts. Be sure you are using the same iCloud account for all of your devices.

- iCloud offers 5 GB of free storage. If you wish to purchase more storage, Apple is happy to sell you more gigabytes.

- For iCloud to backup your photos on your iPhone and iPad, you must turn on the backup feature in Photos. If you don't have enough storage, you will be prompted to upgrade. See below – the iCloud Photo Library cannot be turned on because there is not enough storage available.

- The photos that are in your iCloud library are an exact copy of what is on your phone, iPad and computer (if you use Mac Photos). *When you delete a photo, you are deleting it from all of your devices.*

Other Online or "Cloud" Storage

For people who use PCs, the internet offers "free" cloud storage for photos. We caution our clients about these websites for reasons including:

- With the fast mergers, changes and closures that occur in technology companies, the website may not be around in a few years. We have had clients lose access to their photos because the company closed or merged with another company and service ended for online photo storage.

- A wise saying states that if something is free, you are not the consumer, you are the product. Some "free" sites pay for storing your photos by selling your information or even access to your photos. If you use one of these sites, be sure to review the agreement and make sure you are not signing away the rights to your personal photos.

I wrote this book as a simple guide to saving photos. In order to keep the book short and sweet, I limited a lot of detail in this chapter to the very basics of digital photo organization, a topic worthy of its own guide.

Throughout the book, I have described how we help clients sort their photos. Want to hear how other people pulled their photos together? These stories put into perspective why we do what we do at Pixologie.

Lori's Photo Closet

Our friend Lori has her own successful business helping her clients create beautiful scrapbooks and digital photo books – a calling that she loves. But, something in Lori's house was also calling her – a photo closet full of over 20,000 (our eyeball guesstimate) printed photos that needed to be

scanned before she could create scrapbooks of her family's heritage.

Psychologically, her chaos of photos might as well have been the mountains, so overwhelming it was.

She wrote to us, *"Not only do I have decades of old photos, and take hundreds/thousands of photos each year, but I also acquired heritage photos from my Dad, Pat's parents, and Pat's grandmother dating into the 1800s."*

Here's what she listed in her collection:

- Her father's photo albums (back row on table) – 15+
- Photo boxes with 2400 photos in each of them – 6

- Banker's boxes stuffed full of developed photos and memorabilia – 8
- CDs of photos
- Files and additional boxes filled with photos – 4+
- And many more pictured to the left

As you can see from the photos, Lori's pictures were well organized and ready for scanning.

Frustratingly, Lori stopped scrapbooking because she wanted to back up the only copy of these photos digitally before she put them into albums. With the process being tedious and time-consuming on her flatbed scanner, she was getting further and further behind.

Lori attempted to bring six of the photo boxes to Pixologie to rent our high-speed scanner in the studio. That work didn't even touch the volume of photos she needed to digitize. She then made the decision to rent our scanner in her home for an extended period.

With the Kodak Alaris Picture Saver Scanning System, Lori worked at her pace in the comfort of her own home. She said *"Approaching this project methodically has been helpful. It is not only fine tuning the photo sorting process, it's also helping me get more organized and record family information."* And below you can see how methodical she was with her work station set up in her office.

Lori was very happy to have a fast solution for her photo closet, and she scanned thousands of photos over the course of several weeks.

Eileen's Favorite Memory of Being 83

My mother-in-law Eileen and her niece Susan spent a few hours each week at Pixologie over the course of fourteen months working on a large photo project. First, they sorted through old photos of Susan's side of the family identifying grandparents and great grandparents along with other relatives. Then we helped them scan the photos so they could work on creating a digital photo book of the Kruger/Krueger/Bartelt family history. We loved when Eileen and Susan were in the studio because they laughed so often and clearly enjoyed spending the time together reminiscing.

When Eileen celebrated her 84th birthday earlier this year, and she was asked, "What was your favorite memory from being 83?" After thinking a bit, Eileen replied, "All the time working at Pixologie with Susan and those photos!"

In the photo below, they are working on the last page of their digital photo book. And someday, Susan's granddaughter Grace will treasure looking at the book with her family's history and photos.

That is how photos connect the generations.

A page out of the photo book Eileen and Susan created.

APPENDIX A – About Pixologie

A photo and media organization and management company, Pixologie was founded by Mollie Bartelt and Ann Matuszak because they love photos and the stories that are captured in them. They believe that relationships and lives can be improved when individuals and families celebrate their memories and traditions by looking through their photos together.

Bringing a wealth of non-profit business management, direct sales and social service experience, Ann and Mollie believe photo and media organization services offers

 individuals, families and even organizations and businesses, a place to start and the tools to preserve their photos.

Pixologie, Inc. is located in the greater

Milwaukee, Wisconsin area and is unique in offering photo organization and management services, onsite do-it-yourself options for our clients and trademark licensing for entrepreneurs.

Please contact us for more information. We would love to be a resource for you in your photo and media projects!

Mollie Bartelt

mollieb@pixologieinc.com

Ann Matuszak (Licensing)

annm@pixologieinc.com

Phone: (414) 731-1881

Address: 9803 S. 13th Street, Oak Creek, WI 53154

Website: www.pixologieinc.com

APPENDIX B – Best Practices for Your Memories

When we launched Pixologie in 2013, we had a clear vision of bringing photo organization into a recognized and valued service where consumers can get their stories told and preserved for future generations.

There are too many options for consumers, too many ways to save a photo and too little time to figure it out. Pixologie is changing this by offering clear industry standards for the photo organization and management field and to our licensees who are operating independent businesses.

Over the past two years, we dived deep into developing photo organization standards, digital file format best practices and levels of service.

We have broken down our best practices into Preservation and Archival levels. Following these descriptions, we discuss the Consumer Level of service.

Preservation Level – Generally for consumers, family photo collections

- Printed photos are sorted, stored in photo safe, archival quality boxes
- Scanned photos are 300 or 600 dpi, saved as superior, quality JPGs
- Digital photos are saved as JPGs
- Slides and negatives are scanned at 2000 dpi and saved as JPGs
- Videos and film are transferred to a digital file – MP4
- Back-up includes two digital copies, one onsite (off the main computer) and one offsite

Archival Level – For professional photographers, business and historical photo collections

- Printed photos, slides, negatives are sorted, stored in photo safe, archival quality boxes
- Scanned photos are 600 dpi, saved as TIFFs, once edits completed, can be saved as JPGs
- Digital files are tagged, dates are corrected
- Slides and negatives are scanned at 4000 DPI
- Videos and film are remastered, saved as AVI or MOV
- Back-up includes two digital copies, one onsite (off the main computer) and one offsite

We are committed to educating consumers and our clients on what standards will best preserve their memories for the future. However, these levels of service do come at a higher price point. When we find that clients are looking for a lower cost solution, we have identified an additional level of service – the Consumer Level.

Consumer Level – Many times, people access consumer levels of services because they are unaware there are other options and considerations to ensure their photos and family movies will be around for generations to come. Some consumers do choose to have a lower cost service and are willing to compromise on the quality of service.

- Photos are scanned on flatbed scanners with unknown DPI and quality
- Digital files are saved on DVDs and jump drives with no consideration of how the photo will be organized and found later
- Slides and negatives are scanned using a consumer grade scanner with inconsistent color correction
- Videos and film are transferred to lower size and quality digital formats (MP4s or MPGs) or transferred and compressed straight to a DVD

RESOURCES

Pixologie – A Photo Organization Company

www.pixologieinc.com

Telephone: 414-731-1881

Email: contact@pixologieinc.com

E-Z Photo Scan

www.ezphotoscan.com

Telephone: 866-562-4660

Email: info@ezphotoscan.com

The Association of Personal Photo Organizers

www.appo.com

Find a photo organizer near you

Made in the USA
Las Vegas, NV
03 April 2025

20436501R00059